Tale

of a

Lost Dog

Found

By

Michelle Barrett

and

Karen Magnus

 Blue Dragon Publishing

Published by Blue Dragon Publishing

Williamsburg, VA

www.bluedragon-pub.com

ISBN 978-1-939696-06-9

Cover by Ascent Business Media

*Statistics show that less than 16% of lost dogs
are returned to their rightful owners. This story
is dedicated to the other 84%*

MARCEL

Prologue

My name is Michelle and I'm *that* pet owner who loves their pet as a friend and confidant. That owner-pet connection is a tough thing to explain, yet there is something unique about the connection my dog Marcel and I share. Perhaps it's because we found each other when we needed each other the most. I rescued him from 12 months confinement in a metal crate. He rescued me back by healing my heart after the loss of another beloved dog.

Karen is a friend and fellow dog fanatic who was an integral part of Marcel's new life with me. Karen and I wrote this story together. We wrote it in order to share our experiences of a very specific adventure; but we also wrote it because we have both connected with animals in deep and soulful ways that defy explanation. We invest emotionally in our pets and have done the same with this story.

My name is Karen. As the daughter of a professional dog trainer and all-around animal person who rescued any animal in need, I grew up with a plethora of 4-legged "siblings," pure-bred or rescued, adopted or found. I picked up that passion for nurturing the human-animal interaction and helping both creatures to co-exist peacefully.

Michelle and I started out as co-workers in the Air Force, but a friendship developed as our daily interactions revealed a common work ethic and a similar goal-oriented stubbornness. That friendship grew stronger as we learned of our mutual devotion to our pets.

I was invested in Marcel's adventure because I was Michelle's advisor in his selection, his caregiver when he ran away, and with Michelle when we finally found him. I have been a part of Marcel's entire rescued life and recollecting the events has been therapeutic and educational.

Thank you, for reading our story!

Chapter 1

Dogs have always been a part of my life. But it wasn't until I got my own pup as an adult that I understood the responsibilities that go with truly owning a dog. I knew about the walking, feeding and cleaning tasks that define dog "ownership." What caught me off guard was the heart-consuming, soul-warming responsibility of caring for, protecting and loving these furry, four-legged creatures. They become so much a part of your life that you can't remember life without them or, more significantly, don't want to remember life without them. Somehow, with a wag of their tail and a lick of your face, a dog becomes yours...or rather, you become theirs.

This is the story of dog-love found, lost, regained, lost, and found once more

I got my first dog sight unseen. I was living in California and was on the lookout for a Maltese. I mentioned to my parents in Virginia to keep an eye out for any pups. Before I knew it, my family had picked out the runt of a litter and put her on a plane with a friend flying back to California from the East Coast. I received a telephone update from the ladies' room during her Chicago O'Hare layover to learn that she had "peed on a puppy pad in the bathroom stall."

When they made it to California and I finally laid eyes on the 2-pound poof of soft white hair, I fell in love. I crouched down and held out my arms and instantly, she was running at me with innocent enthusiasm. Her tiny legs ran her body to me, eager to satisfy any curiosity about this newest human in her circle of friends.

Violating my own rule about dogs earning their name, Q-Tip was Q-Tip before my parents even knew I was searching for a dog. I knew I wanted a Maltese, having grown up with one, and my uncle had a Maltese named "Cotton," so "Q-Tip" seemed apropos for Cotton's cousin. Q-Tip was my beautiful Maltese and a very independent little girl. She loved being around people, and she needed people—as would be expected of a pet, but she had a stubborn streak. She was happy to learn and please, but at the same time she was willfully her own master, leading to numerous lessons in "Who's the boss?"

I took Q-tip everywhere. She rode on my shoulders in the car, sat in my lap in the house, lay at my feet when I worked and even made a few trips to the office with me. Her frequent coast-to-coast airline flights to see "Grama" and "Papa" even caused me to have a serious conversation with my airline of choice about getting my dog a frequent flyer card (I suggested they give her half miles for every mile flown). I figured it was a reasonable request considering how much I spent to have her as my carry on.

Q-Tip was a Godsend. She was my tangible family while miles separated me from my parents and siblings. She moved with me from California to Texas, Alabama, DC, Rhode Island and back to DC. She comforted me through a break-up, helped me transition to a self-employed life, and welcomed me like Fred Flintstone's Dino after frustrating days at work. She was more than a pet, she was my child, and I rapidly socialized the "dog-ter" moniker (instead of "daughter") with my own family.

When she was ready to play, she hunkered down on her front legs like a linebacker waiting for the snap. She hopped from side-to-side, daring you to catch her. Her agile body allowed her to sneak through unperceivable cracks in our backyard fence. Despite makeshift fixes to contain her by covering escape holes with bricks, tree stumps, wooden shingles or even a wagon, she always managed to pinch her 4-pound frame out of the yard.

One pattern of breakouts in our Alabama home involved tunneling out of our yard, crossing the street and tunneling *into* a neighbor's yard. The neighbor's youngest was an 11-year-old girl named Desiree, thrilled to have Q-Tip as a baby sister. Q-Tip's tunneling dyed her white hair red with Alabama's sienna soil, so Desiree would bathe, blow dry and brush Q-Tip and then dress her in doll clothes. The first time this happened, Q-Tip was busy playing spa while I was frantically scouring the neighborhood for my baby girl.

I had come home from work to an empty house, a sickening change in my routine, which included an eager greeting from Q-Tip that would make loyal Dino look sluggish. The muggy Alabama day had succumbed to an evening storm of slanted rain, lightning fireworks and bone-rattling rumbles of thunder. I drove through the suburban streets calling for Q-Tip through my open car windows. The only attention I attracted was that of helpful neighbors who bolstered my search by covering more ground than I could alone. Their door-to-door efforts led me right to my own neighbor who opened his door to reveal Desiree's blooming pet spa business.

Anytime spa time happened after that, it was because Q-Tip needed a bath; so with the neighbor parents' approval, I'd let Q-Tip into their backyard, wait a few hours and then pick up Q-Tip, freshly bathed and combed, and wearing some accessory belonging to one of Desiree's dolls.

Because I saw Q-Tip as "people," I didn't socialize her enough as a dog, sheltering her from dogs many times her size rather than helping her learn the doggy etiquette that allows dogs as diverse as wolfhounds and teacup poodles to interact predictably. As a result, when she "greeted" other dogs, she did so with a headlong sprint, unaware that her eagerness had a threatening interpretation, despite her light weight. And that eager greeting was ultimately her downfall.

Chapter 2

At the young age of 9, Q-Tip ran to greet a dog much bigger than her. The bigger dog responded to her exuberance with his own instinctive reaction of picking Q-Tip up in his jaws and flinging her against landscaping pavers. The bruising was immediate and sickeningly visible against her normally pink skin. Our regular vet released her with some pain medication and I sat with her on our couch afraid that even a gentle pet could inflict more pain. Through all her pain, she longed only to be by my side. She restlessly fidgeted to find comfort but always found a position where her body rested against me. I cradled her gingerly, unsure if my embrace was relieving any pressure on her swollen body.

For almost an hour, I stared at her discolored belly, unable to remember its normal innocent pink color. I tried to envision the confusion of emotions through which her body had tumbled. Excitement, fear and pain, followed by chemically induced relief.

Not feeling qualified enough to care for her should something happen, and wanting a second opinion on whether my dog should have been sent home, I brought her to SouthPaws Veterinary Specialists & Emergency Center, where they strongly recommended I leave her overnight for observation and better pain medication.

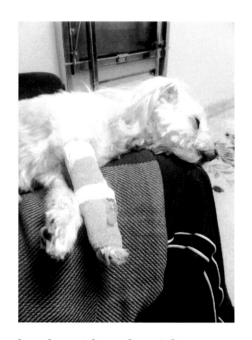

Although I hated to be without her, I knew she needed professional care and not just my compassionate attention. She lay on my lap with a dainty pink wrap around her right arm securing her IV line. She was already comfortably sedated with medicine and I trusted the doctors to care for her as if she was their own. With a reassuring, "We'll call you if we notice anything," I left my dear companion at the emergency hospital.

When the phone rang at 2:38 in the morning, it didn't have a chance to finish its first ring before I picked it up. It was the vet. I couldn't think of one positive reason an emergency room veterinarian would call at 2:38 in the morning and my breath and heart stopped while I waited for him to prove me wrong.

"Q-Tip coded," he said.

I'd watched enough melodrama on TV to know that this wasn't an encouraging medical phrase.

"What happened?" was all I asked.

"We don't know. We got her heart started again but our nurse is breathing for her. It would probably be best for you to get here as soon as possible to see her."

Because the call was on my cell phone, I was already in the car. It should have been obvious what the final outcome of that early morning trip was going to be, but I refused to accept it and prayed fervently on the car ride to the hospital—a short ride in miles, but an eternity in time away from my girl.

The vet pulled me into a waiting room attempting to explain what had happened. It wasn't something anyone could have really explained to me in my state and he seemed just as surprised by the turn of events. She was only there for observation, so her sudden decline and the CPR they had to give her wasn't expected. Q-Tip's internal injuries were much greater than any of the vets had realized. Though they were able to get her heart started when she coded, he reminded me that there was a nurse with a ventilator bag breathing for her. His monotone words were an attempt to prepare me for what my dog would look like.

Through the swinging door marked "Authorized Personnel Only," I entered the antiseptic area as announced by the overpowering reek of alcohol and the muted chimes of medical monitoring devices. The staff of four had only one high-priority patient, my Q-Tip. While other animals slumbered in drug-induced dreams, Q-Tip lay on a cold metal table in the center of the room. The green screen readout by her side replayed her rapid heartbeat as the nurse continued to puff air into Q-Tip's body. Her body was alive, but her open eyes were...lifeless. It was a gut-wrenching, sickening feeling to see her there and the memory of that sight still haunts me. I stared at her vacant eyes, afraid to think of how much suffering she had already endured. Though her heart fought on, I knew she was gone and letting her go was the right and humane thing to do.

The nurse continued to puff air while I stared in disbelief, stroking Q-Tip's soft white hair, crying my apologies and final goodbyes. I still couldn't fathom that my little girl was in this condition. I thanked her for 9 wonderful years, telling her how proud I was, how happy she had made me, how grateful I was that she had been a part of my life and that she had let me be a part of hers. I was crushed, feeling that I had failed her so miserably that after a brief 9 years together, she was about to leave me.

My head throbbed as I nodded to the doctor, who was patient and compassionate as he injected the fluid into Q-Tip's IV. My vision was blurred by tears, and my body bristled from an overdose of emotion. Within seconds after the syringe had emptied, the doctor touched my arm, telling me that my Q-

Tip had crossed the rainbow bridge. Sobs overtook my numb body. My legs trembled, threatening to give up their job of supporting me. I could not believe the finality of Q-Tip's death, could not believe it was her warm but lifeless body I stroked.

Despite being surrounded by dear friends who had unhesitatingly given up their own sleep to be there next to me, I felt hollow and alone. The only feeling I had was a tingling sensation in my skin as my body heaved with sobs of loss. I loved Q-Tip so much. I had tried my best to care for her, to the point of spoiling her, but it hadn't kept her with me.

In less than 24 hours, I was picking up Q-Tip's ashes and choosing a nice wooden urn for her. The next few days were depressing. I didn't think I'd ever get back to normal, I wasn't sure I ever wanted to feel normal, and I felt guilty in those brief interludes of feeling normal. Unsure if it was the smartest choice, I stayed home from work. The stillness and quiet at home was a steady reminder of the new normal in my life, but I wasn't ready to deal with work and coworkers' sympathy. Everything around the house had "her" on it. Her smell, her fur, her memory.

Chapter 3

I was so heartbroken over Q-Tip's death that the thought of ever getting another dog was nowhere near my conscious thoughts. I knew there would be a day in my distant future when I would eventually get another dog, but at the time I couldn't imagine life with any dog but her. I had put so much of myself into Q-Tip and our relationship that it didn't seem fair to put any other dog in the shadow of who Q-Tip had been to me.

But it happened. Far sooner than I thought it would. And quite frankly, it happened a lot sooner than my friends thought it should have. Like many things in life, events started unfolding before I realized what was really going on. Within a month, I was randomly surfing the web for combinations of "Brussels Griffon" and "Northern Virginia," just to fill my time—not really expecting to find anything that could interest me, and certainly not intending to pursue anything that might come up so soon. Looking at other dogs felt like cheating, much like dating *the day after* a breakup.

But two Brussels brothers, Tiger and Timmy, came through my breed and location filters. Having a long-standing infatuation with tigers, seeing a dog named Tiger triggered some immediate connection, and despite my grief over Q-Tip, somehow this little Brussels named Tiger called to me. I just had to go see these dogs. I didn't plan on taking one home, but I felt compelled to go see them. The dogs were in foster care through Caring Hearts Rescue after being saved from a puppy mill. Undeterred by the seven-page application required to see the foster pups, I started the dog rescue process.

One week after seeing the dogs on the internet, I was at the foster home looking at the boys. My focus was on Tiger as I was a bit turned off, to be honest, with Timmy's under bite and seemingly suspicious look. Both boys were still on weight-gain recovery and were very skittish from their poor treatment at the puppy mill. I brought my friend Karen along as I prepared to meet the dogs I'd only seen online. I needed the company and her expertise.

In all her nervous excitement, and yet still anxious about getting another dog so soon, Michelle asked me to come with her to see Tiger and Timmy. She wanted moral support from another dog lover, but also the less emotional perspective of someone with years of experience training dogs and doing rescue work. I had seen up close how devastated Michelle was when she lost Q-tip, and I knew that even though she was still grieving that loss, only she would know when she was ready to connect with another dog.

My goal was to help her be objective and to understand exactly what she might be signing up for if she decided to adopt one of these maltreated Brussels brothers. We talked to the foster mom to learn about both of the dogs and her observations of their individual personalities. She relayed that they would only approach humans from behind and advised against making direct eye contact with them. But they had bonded with their foster mom and I read that to indicate they had an amazing willingness to learn and trust humans in spite of their dubious first year with our species.

We had taken little baggies of cheese and liverwurst to use in our efforts to engage with the two pups who were not very willing to interact with anyone other than their foster mom. Once the foster mom felt comfortable with us, she watched us from a spot where the Brussels could not see her. Michelle and I sat on the ground and observed as much as they would let us, and fed these two skittish little boys. It soon became apparent to me that even though Tiger was the more handsome of the two, and the one with the name that had drawn Michelle to come see them, he was the least willing to connect with us. Timmy on the other hand was already showing signs, not of trust, but at least of willingness to investigate us, associate with us (albeit very carefully) and try to figure out how he could get us to deliver more of the delicious treats we had with us.

As we sat on the ground quietly working with the two, I told Michelle that I believed if she decided to take one of the boys, it would be better if she chose Timmy. I explained that with their backgrounds, to become the type of dog she wanted—one that could go everywhere and socialize with all sorts of people and other animals—she would need one that had a shot at making a recovery from their skittish beginnings. I knew Michelle's very social lifestyle would require a companion that could eventually transition to something resembling a balanced dog—maybe not 100%, but close. In our 2 hours interacting with these dogs it became clear that Timmy had possibilities. I explained that Tiger might progress as well, but that he would do so faster once Timmy was no longer in the picture, because Timmy was the dominant brother. But because Tiger was not very willing to engage with us or explore possibilities with us, Timmy was the better bet for her.

I also told Michelle it would take a lot of work and patience, and that there would be many challenges, but that I thought she was up to it if she decided to go forward. One of the many things I recognized in Michelle was her stubborn persistence to make things work. If anything, my sympathies were for Timmy, knowing that no one would push him toward recovery harder than Michelle. Timmy had already shown some tentative interest in interacting with Michelle more than anyone else there that day. I think he knew that she was the one he might spend more time with if he made friends. And sure enough, Michelle decided that she had to have Timmy, even though he was not the one she initially came to see. I can't tell you how many times I have witnessed rescue animals meeting their new people for the first time. They seem to know instinctively that this is their future and embrace it very quickly.

Before I realized what was happening, I was setting in motion the plans to adopt Timmy, the Brussels Griffon with an under bite and suspicious glare; and the one who had eaten liverwurst so greedily that he wore more than he ate.

I coordinated a half-day of work on the day Timmy was to come home to live with me. I was pretty distracted all morning as I belatedly questioned whether I had rushed into this decision. This wasn't a new puppy I could mold, but a 13-month old dog who had spent his life in a kennel and came with baggage I wasn't sure I was qualified to handle.

Timmy and his foster mom, Pat, beat me to my house so I rushed to park my car in the driveway, sprinting to the van to meet them. Timmy was probably just as scared as I was, meeting for our first date. Pat coaxed the dog out from the van and walked him on a slack leash. He seemed neither excited to come to his new home nor anxious to get back in the van. I'm sure running toward an already-nervous dog wasn't the smartest approach to exhibit on day one, yet it was the behavior dictated by my excitement. I wanted to share the moment. I looked up and saw my neighbor and friend Bonnie watching the new dog's arrival. I pointed at Timmy and I could see my exhilaration reflected in her expression.

Pat led Timmy to the house and we headed to the backyard. Part of the protocol with transitioning a foster pup to his forever home was making sure the dog understood that the foster home was a part of his past and this new place and new human was now his new home and family.

I sat on the back deck while Pat picked up Timmy and put him in my arms. He lay in my arms on his back, like a baby, belly exposed, in a pose of trusting comfort. We locked eyes. And then the boy melted my heart as he gazed up at me, sighed away his past and trusted me, his new home and his new life enough to drift off to sleep.

True to his online photo, Timmy had long, spindly little legs, too long for his thin body. When he sat, his back arched with an aloof slouch. His petite face was a cross between Chewbacca, an Ewok, and Paddington the Bear. He had an under bite and his long tongue stuck out of his recessed face. Now that little boy with a former life of neglect and abuse as a puppy mill number was mine. And as he drifted off to sleep in my arms that first day, he left that life behind him. And with that new life came a new name.

My first viewing of the Brussels brothers online launched a name-the-dog daydream. I decided that if one of these Brussels were mine, I would name him "Marcel" after the capuchin monkey in the TV show *Friends*.

Timmy was the dog in the photo. The dog softly snoring in my arms was Marcel. A new dog for me, a new name for him; we were both starting over. In my arms I held hope for love and healing. Cradling him were arms that promised safety, trust and a better life.

The rest of the day Marcel was either by my side or on my lap. We were attached from that first moment; tethered at the heart, connected by the soul. If you've never felt that connection with a person or an animal, it's difficult to explain. If you've been fortunate enough to experience it, it's impossible to forget.

Marcel and I continued to click just as we had when Pat put him in my arms. Karen and her mom were both on speed dial and also replied to my almost-daily e-mails. Karen guided me through dog-training feedback sessions each day over coffee at work. She and her mom had taught me about clicker training before I had even decided to get another dog and I was running Marcel through the wringer with nightly clicker sessions. Within a couple weeks, Marcel could sit, high-five, wave and lay down.

But he wasn't motivated by food. He responded to praise from me more than any tasty kibble I put in front of him. When I talked to him, he looked back at me and, while I knew he couldn't understand my words, I knew that what he cherished was the one-on-one attention we had with each other.

He had zero interest in stuffed animals or chew toys. I suppose that in a puppy mill, where someone viewed him as merely an employee to make more puppies, he wasn't afforded toys and chew-things. He received a lot of welcome-home dog gifts but he treated them as just an obstacle on the ground to walk around, not as something that should be gnawed on, thrown or fetched.

Our biggest hurdle was his fear of the car. Again, as a puppy mill number, I don't suppose he got a lot of car rides to the park. But in this new life, car rides were essential because taking him everywhere I could was part of what I considered normal. So with more phone calls to Karen, we worked out a tedious plan to get him used to the car. Marcel and I logged many garage miles just sitting in the car with the door open, eating dinner together in the car, listening to the car radio and eventually graduating to a road trip down the driveway and back. But within 3 weeks, he was jumping in the car in order to sit on my lap and be with me wherever that vehicle took us.

And just as we were making progress, only 29 days after Marcel and I had become a family, I had to go on a 3-day work trip down to Robins Air Force Base in Georgia. I debated where to leave him while I was gone, terrified of every option because none of them included him and me together. I briefly toyed with the idea of bringing him along. In the end, I opted to leave him with Karen and her husband Robert, since Karen was a dog trainer and Robert was home during the day.

Robert was a kind and caring man who put up with my and Karen's doting on dogs. Karen knew how much this dog meant to me, since she'd played a big part in selecting him, and she was training me just as much as she was training Marcel. Their daughter Isabel had also inherited the animal-affection gene and I knew it would be healthy for Marcel to be exposed to younger people. Marcel would have one-on-one time with Robert during the day while Isabel was at school and then Marcel could learn to play with Isabel as Robert supervised. One thing was for sure: Marcel would not be starved for attention while with Karen, Robert and Isabel.

I dropped Marcel off with Robert as late as I could on Monday morning to make my flight out of DC that afternoon. Robert was patient as he reassured me that Marcel would benefit from some male bonding time and that he would take good care of him. I knew Marcel would be fine, but I was still sad to leave my boy, unable to explain to him why I was leaving and that I'd be back, but I knew he'd be in good hands.

Marcel's first day and night at our house were unexciting. He did well, followed us around, and was happy to hop into our laps whenever we sat down. His only distress seemed to come from interaction with our 10-year old daughter, Isabel. Not because of anything she did, but just her presence in general. She is high energy and exuberant and we had to keep reminding her that for Marcel it was unnerving when she moved quickly or was noisy. Isabel has spent her life around a multitude of animals, many of which were rescues, and she has inherited her parents' love for all animals. So she tried hard to curb her enthusiasm, wanting desperately for Marcel to like her. As the evening progressed, Marcel seemed to be taking this little venture in stride.

The initial part of my trip was uneventful; rental car, hotel room, dinner at a restaurant, first day of meetings and so on. I was anxious to Skype with Karen and Marcel later that night or the next day. It may seem a ridiculous thing to do but if you *have* had that connection, you've probably not only Skyped, but set up a Facebook page and e-mail account for your pet as well.

Karen and I talked on the phone, and I was reassured Marcel had fared well on his first night without me. Our Skype date was set up for the next evening around 6:00.

When Karen's call came in around 5:30, earlier than we had planned, I was thrilled. When I heard her voice, I was suspicious.

"Hi, Michelle," came the tentative voice.

Cautiously, I returned the greeting.

"Michelle," her voice was shaky. "Marcel ran away and we haven't found him yet."

Chapter 4

I dropped to my knees. Guilt flowed as if Q-Tip's ghost haunted me with this punishment for getting a replacement dog so soon. I argued with the taunting thought; Marcel was more than just a replacement. My little man, having been plucked from a crate that was his 24/7 home for more than a year, spending 2 weeks in foster care, 29 days with me, then just 1 day with another family, had bolted.

The 700 miles between Marcel and me might as well have been 7,000. On top of Q-Tip's loss, this was a blow I didn't think I could stand.

It was 4:30 on Tuesday afternoon, Marcel's second day with us, when my phone rang at work. It was Robert. His words tumbled out in his distress. "Come home now. Marcel ran away. I tried to catch him, but he ran straight to the school and under the fence and into the woods."

I was momentarily stunned and horrified all at once. So many questions tumbled through my head, but staying on the phone at that moment was not going to get me home, so I said, "I'm leaving right now. I'll call you as soon as I get off the bus."

Washington DC's excellent mass transit system makes up for the city's notoriously terrible traffic. So rather than drive to work, I ride a commuter bus where phone calls are not considered part of the protocol, so I had to wait until I got to the lot where my car was parked to call Michelle. I raced out of the Pentagon, sprinted to the bus stop and jumped on a bus that was just about to depart. I suffered through the next 30 minutes anxiously stewing about getting home to find Marcel, and dying inside because I knew I would have to call Michelle and tell her what had happened. And what exactly *had* happened? I was completely at a loss. We had a fenced back yard, and we had not been letting Marcel go out by himself. One of us was always keeping an eye on him. We did not take him out in the front yard, where it was unfenced, for fear of this very scenario. I stared at my cell phone, knowing Robert would text me if there were any updates.

I got off the bus and got in my car. Having received no new information from Robert, I dialed Michelle, cringing at the thought I was about to blow her world to bits.

Karen filled me in on the details, little of which I caught. Robert and Marcel were best of buds, or so it seemed until he seized an opportunity to bolt toward...what? Where would he go? To the "house" he'd known for a year? To the place where he was first treated with love? To the life he and I had spent a mere 29 days establishing? Was he afraid or was it just an adventure to him? All that mattered to me was he was gone. Despite being aware I could never really know why he ran, I prayed and hoped for an opportunity to ask him.

Marcel was last seen at a school down the street from them. There was a gap in the schoolyard fence, and Robert had watched Marcel sprint through that gap at breakneck speed. That was the last he'd seen of my little man. Karen told me they would keep looking and do everything else they could to ensure he was found.

Our conversation was quick and tearful, but as action-oriented women, neither one of us wanted to waste precious minutes crying when there was a dog to be found.

After calling Michelle, I phoned Robert on my way to the house. At last I was able to ask some of the questions rolling around my head to get to the bottom of how this had happened. Robert had picked up Isabel from school at 3:30 as usual and everything was fine. Robert and Isabel began their after-school routine with Marcel following Robert. Robert opened the kitchen door that led to the garage and realized he had not closed the garage door when he and Isabel had returned home. Marcel also noticed and, at that moment, did something completely unexpected. He dashed through the middle of Robert's legs and sprinted into the garage and out the door.

Having taken off his shoes when he got home, Robert was sock-footed as he followed Marcel, praying hard that he would not run off. Marcel had gone into the front yard and was sniffing around. Robert knew not to chase, run, or in any way startle Marcel, so he did not try to catch him, knowing that would only make

Marcel run, or at least dance out of reach. He walked slowly nearer, then sat down on the ground and talked to Marcel. At first Marcel appeared interested in coming to Robert; he circled him a couple of times like he might approach. Then Robert saw a look pass over Marcel's face and he knew Marcel was going to bolt. And bolt he did. He ran as if every demon he could imagine were on his heels. Straight down our street to the elementary school, now with Robert running, still shoeless, in hot pursuit. When Marcel reached the school he went to the far side of the huge playing field. The field was fenced, but at the farthest corner there was a gap underneath big enough for a small animal to crawl under. Robert entered the field, but was unable to get near because Marcel's long legs had covered the half mile in lightning-fast time. He saw Marcel run the fence line one time, discover the space at the corner, and duck under. Still at full speed, Marcel ran into the forest on the other side.

Robert raced back to the house and called me. He, too, knew how much Michelle adored this dog, and was physically ill that Marcel had escaped while under his care. Isabel was in tears and wanted to help look for him too.

I knew there was a flurry of activity already in place in Virginia, but I felt helpless in Georgia. Still leveled to my knees by the news, I prayed. Prayed that my dog would be safe. Prayed that my dog would be comforted. Prayed that my dog wouldn't be scared. Prayed that my dog would be found. And as I prayed, an overpowering feeling possessed me. It was certainly not a feeling of calm, but more of a sense that this would end well. I didn't know how, I didn't know when, but I knew it would be ok. Despite that sense, I needed someone to tell me it would be okay.

I called my partner Jen, stationed in England, to tell her the news. Hearing the story relayed in my own voice only enforced my disbelief. She felt helpless being so far away. But I needed someone to tell me it would be okay. I needed to hear those words. I didn't care if she meant it or believed it; I just needed to hear her say it.

Not willing to sit idle, determined to do all I could despite being geographically distant, I logged onto my work laptop, thankful for free and fast hotel wireless internet access. I opened up Microsoft Word and made a quick "Lost" flyer, grateful that I had accumulated plenty of pictures of my dog even though I'd only had him for 29 days. I found out later that posting "lost dog" posters increased the chances of a successful reunion by 200%. I e-mailed the flyer to Karen and Robert and the local Stafford SPCA, who were instrumental in making the notification go viral.

LOST

Very skittish...call with a calm voice.

Last seen by Swans Creek Elem. Dumfries, VA

June 7, 2011

My friend created a Craigslist ad while I updated my Facebook status, trying to get the word out every way I could. I posted a picture of Marcel on my page and tagged my friends who were anywhere near Dumfries so the photo and information would re-post on their pages, in the hope that their friends with whom I might not be connected would be aware and on the lookout.

> Michelle Barrett
>
> My luck with dogs continues...Marcel has escaped from his sitters and there's a neighborhood search party going on. Last seen by Swans Creek Elementary School in Dumfries, VA. Requesting prayers from my FB fam.
>
> Like · Comment · 7 June at 18:35

Right after I posted the status update, a friend of a friend posted that she was willing to help out since she lived in Dumfries. Her offer to help accompanied a flood of electronic confirmations of prayers, positive thoughts and availability to join in the search. It was merely the beginning of the outpouring of support, encouragement and help I would get in my search. Karen and Robert already formed a search party that was headquartered at the school where Marcel was last seen. I continued to get calls from friends who wanted to help, but despite—or maybe because of—my helplessness being so far away, I hated to impose on people to look for *my* dog, *my* responsibility.

Chapter 5

My more persistent friends didn't ask, they just told me they were going. My next-door neighbor Steve was one of them. He just headed south with no specific address, then called and told me it'd be best if I just passed him the actual coordinates. I knew Steve well enough to know not to fight it. I gave him the school address and Karen's cell phone number, and then passed Steve's digits to her, along with the news that the search party was growing. Before I knew it, my neighbors, my friends and family members were en route to Dumfries, enduring DC metro traffic and the I-95 corridor to get there to look for *my* boy. The warmth of all the support soothed the emptiness and pain that numbed my body.

The first day and night of our search for Marcel began with Robert going onto the other side of the fence near the spot where Marcel ducked under and searching in the woods for any sign of Marcel. When he finally returned, he was covered in debris, spider webs, ticks and assorted other insect wildlife. The forest behind the school was thick and hard to move around in because the trees were close together and the terrain was rough. Our neighbor, also a dog lover, drove around the forest to a road called Possum Point that sandwiched the forest with the school. She and her son drove up and down it for about an hour looking and calling, but with no result.

Robert and I walked all over the area calling out Marcel's name, uncertain which direction he might have gone and, therefore, not sure which side of the woods he may have exited. Meanwhile Michelle's family and friends were responding to her electronic postings and were appearing at our place and at the school to help in the search. We had people fan out and search the woods, others drove up and down the roads that bordered the forest, while still others went door-to-door talking to anyone they saw, asking them to keep an eye out for Marcel.

Eventually I had to send Robert and Isabel home. Isabel had to go to school the next day and Robert was tired, dirty, thirsty, hungry, and so distressed he needed to do something else for a little bit. I stayed out with many of Michelle's friends and family long after dark. We set up temporary camp in the school parking lot and had a feeding station set up at the spot where Marcel had gone under the fence.

The "Lost" flyer was out and making its rounds on the Internet, being printed and plastered around the neighborhood. Marcel's picture was up on Facebook, tagged and re-tagged, posted and re-posted. The prayer network was in surge mode and I felt that I had done all I could at that moment. Not being there in Dumfries looking for Marcel was killing me. My heart threw itself against my rib cage with each anxious beat, my eyes were swollen from an over-productive tear factory and my head pounded from trying to answer "Why?"

Unsure of what to do next, or what I *could* do next, I logged onto Google Maps and used the satellite view to zoom in on the elementary school that was host to Marcel's last sighting. I stared at the screen, naively expecting to see my little brown dog darting around the grass in seen-from-space miniature. My connection with Marcel was strong enough that I felt as if I could will him back to that area where so many people awaited his return.

Emotionless, I turned on the TV for some background distraction as I waited for calls or texts on my phone and monitored my Facebook page and e-mail accounts. It was June of 2011 and the Casey Anthony trial was in full swing. I hadn't followed the case much, but I knew it revolved around a once-missing child and a young mother. Except for the "young" part, I figured she and I might have something in common. I listened to the recap of the day's trial and learned all I needed to know about this young mother—she was guilty. In 4 hours, I had done more to find a dog I had had for only 29 days than she had done in 31 days for a child she'd had for 2 years.

My phone rang and snapped me out of my self-imposed jury duty. It was my only connection to Marcel and all those out there looking for him, so I was on hyper alert and perilously close to exceeding my phone plan's data and cellular minutes. It was Stephanie, another neighbor, but not just a neighbor— she was our veterinarian and a very good friend. Stephanie had been another key advisor to Marcel and me during our first month together. She brought in medical and behavioral expertise to augment Karen's guidance.

After working her 12-hour shift, Stephanie and her dog Scooter headed down to Dumfries to link up with the search posse. Marcel and Scooter had become fast friends and were near twins with their size, fur coloring and trot-like gait. Stephanie thought maybe Scooter could lure Marcel out of the woods and back to his forever home. So as the sun set and the larger search party started to call it a night, Stephanie and Scooter joined Karen and Steve.

When Stephanie and Scooter arrived at the school, we walked together to where Marcel was last seen. Quietly we strained our eyes and ears for any sight or sound that could be Marcel. Whether it was wishful thinking or something else making the noise, we thought we heard the sound of Marcel's tags tinkling several times. We persuaded Scooter to go under the fence and explore on the other side in the hope that a familiar dog face might encourage Marcel, if he was there, to come out of hiding. But though Stephanie and I spent quite a while on this activity, we had no results. We even tried having Michelle on speaker phone attempting to call Marcel, thinking that if he were there and heard her voice he might come out where we could at least see him.

Eventually, around midnight, I had to leave and get some rest. I had to go to work the next day and I'd been searching for Marcel since I had made it home. I hadn't been able to eat, my appetite gone in my anguish over Marcel. At this point, I was not sure who I was more anguished over, Marcel or Michelle. I knew from my own experience many years ago, when my beloved Yellow Lab jumped a six-foot fence in her desperation to get away from the neighbor's fireworks, how emotionally devastating it is to lose your beloved pet in such a fashion. My Lab disappeared into the night, and it was 36 hours later before I recovered her, after a massive search. I remembered my emotional nightmare and knew that Michelle was going through something equivalent, but worse...she was in another state far away and unable to get here, and I knew she felt helpless and ill from the worry. I left, but Stephanie and Steve assumed the reins of the graveyard search shift, still keeping a watchful eye at the school as I headed home to attempt to sleep.

I was getting constant text updates from Stephanie and Steve. They camped out in the school field with full bladders and empty stomachs, enduring mosquito bites and pitch-blackness. The ground and still air released the solar powered heat of the sun that had set hours earlier. The policeman who came to kick them off the field for their illegal presence on school property after hours was sympathetic to their search and allowed them to stay. Each time Stephanie or Steve heard what they hoped was the jingle of Marcel's dog tags, she called me and put me on speaker phone to let me call for Marcel. Sometimes Scooter would alert and Stephanie thought maybe he smelled or heard Marcel and she would place another phone call to me in my desolate Marcel Search Satellite Headquarters in Georgia.

Each time the phone rang, I hoped it was *THE* call and prayed it wasn't *that* call. The knot in my stomach was the disappointment of letting my boy down, for bringing him to my home and promising that his life would be better than it had been when he was confined to a kennel for every minute of his day. I tried to empathize with him, sensing his fear and worry out there in the dark, lonely, unfamiliar woods. I prayed he would know, somehow sense, that I still loved him, and hoped he could hear the many people calling out for him, assuming he knew his name was now "Marcel," even if he was afraid to go to those voices.

I lay in my Georgia hotel room bed, feeling guilty for any physical comfort the pillow, the soft mattress or the cool air conditioner brought me, knowing Marcel was thirsty, hungry, frightened, exhausted and over-heated. This was summer in DC, humid and hot with little air movement to bring any relief.

Stephanie was diligent with her text message updates; even if they were just to say they hadn't heard anything. But around 2:00 in the morning on Wednesday, she called to let me know that since she and Steve both had to work later that morning, they probably should start the 30-minute drive back up to Falls Church. I could hardly blame them. I was amazed they had even done all that they had. I was, and still am, ever grateful for the strength of my friendships. Stephanie comforted me with a vet's opinion that Marcel was most likely hunkered down for the night and would benefit from the rest, however slight, he could get.

I hoped and prayed that Marcel would get sleep because it was surely eluding me that night. Guilt, hurt, stress and isolation robbed me of any ability to get comfortable enough to rest, even though I knew my body and mind needed it more than ever. But something else plagued me: the bigger question of what "life lesson" this was supposed to teach me. Why was I being put through such heartache? Had I really done anything to deserve this? What was my take-away? I had given Q-Tip a great life and she was taken away from me way too early. I had rescued Marcel from what I considered to be an empty existence and treated him like he was the center of the universe. I didn't understand what I had done wrong and for what pet crime I was being punished.

The next morning I knew that going to work was pointless. I hadn't slept and still hadn't eaten, and so I contacted my boss to tell him that I wanted to stay home and search for Marcel. Permission was immediately granted. Fortunately for Michelle and me, we work with other animal lovers and they understood that until the situation was resolved we would be inconsolable. So by 6 a.m. Wednesday, I was back out at the school searching for signs of Marcel as I turned over in my mind what next steps should be taken in our search.

Around 6:00 that morning, I checked my e-mail, Facebook and phone for any messages I might not have heard come in while I floated in and out of stunned contemplation. Nothing. I was afraid to bug any of my friends who had already done so much to look for my dog.

I had to remember that I was there for work and there was a whole day of meetings ahead of me. It *might* have been possible to do if I could have had access to my phone, but our meetings involved confidential information and no electronic devices would be allowed nearby. There was a brief moment when I fooled myself into thinking I could pull it off, that it was just a dog and destiny would carry out its outcome whatever it was...but it was brief. My belief about destiny is that you have to at least meet it halfway. So if finding my dog was important to me, then I had to be in Virginia, not in Georgia. My mind would not be engaged in anything work-related while Marcel was missing and while my friends were doing the tasks that were my responsibility.

Fortunately, I worked with and worked for dog lovers, not just dog *owners*. I was on the trip with my immediate supervisor, an Air Force Colonel who, after seeing my swollen, tear-drained eyes, had no hesitation allowing me to go home and covering for me in our meetings. Back at the Pentagon was another Colonel who helped me arrange my trip back home. Usually a frugal person, money was no object for me in my itinerary change. I was fortunate to have dog lovers on the other ends of the phone calls I made to change my flight and schedule a bus to get to the Atlanta airport more than an hour away. Their empathetic understanding fortified my decision to return to Virginia to look for Marcel.

> Michelle's news that she was coming home early and heading straight to my house to join the search was a moment of both relief and dread. I was relieved because I knew that Marcel might respond to her when he might not respond to anyone else, but I dreaded looking into her eyes and seeing her pain, knowing that we would likely still not have found Marcel by the time she got there.

My friends at Warner Robins Air Force Base were kind enough to drop everything they were doing to help me on my path back to

Virginia. Beth found me an office where I could cry out my story as I explained my situation to the shuttle service, travel agency and airline. Steph monitored the saga on Facebook and left work to pick me up and drive me to a bus station an hour away. Roberta waited with me until my ride to the bus station arrived, sending me off with a hug and well wishes. It was a powerful display of the depths of friendships my Air Force career had afforded me, not just there in Georgia, but around the globe.

My Air Force family in Virginia was displaying that same depth of caring. Beth, a co-worker turned friend from a previous assignment, was notorious for living on a night owl's schedule. She took a day off from work and was up at an hour closer to when she was usually just calling it a night. While Beth was neither a pet owner or pet lover, she was still down in Dumfries with Karen posting flyer, re-posting flyers people had removed and interrogating every pedestrian who might have been witness to a Marcel sighting.

Another Air Force friend, Tracy, had her family in town and was prepared to bring the whole lot of them to Dumfries to help look for my boy. But still afraid of having too many unfamiliar voices scaring him back into hiding, I took her up on an even more helpful task. Tracy taxied my neighbor Bonnie and my niece Ally to Washington National airport so that when I landed, the two of them could jump in my car and we could legally take the High Occupancy Vehicle lane. This was critical as my estimated airport arrival time was at the peak of DC rush hour traffic—this was no time to be driving in the 2 MPH lane.

I boarded my flight in Atlanta, dreading the 2 hours I would be out of contact with the search. The wheels had barely touched down and cleared the active runway when I turned on my cell phone, praying there would be a text about Marcel being found. Nothing.

I had Michelle's friend, Beth, whom I had just met that morning, with me while Michelle was making her way home. We were in full swing in the search. We were plastering every neighborhood surface with flyers if we thought there was even the remotest chance Marcel might have visited the area.

Robert took care of our animals, dropped Isabel at school and then alerted all the staff at the school to the search. Flyers were given to all the teachers and staff who also were quick to find ways to help in the search. Once Robert left the school he joined in the search on foot by going back into the woods behind the school to begin methodically figuring out all the possible ways Marcel might have traveled based on where an animal could pass through and where not.

Beth and I traveled every road we could think of, handing out and hanging up flyers. We talked to every person we saw and even went into businesses in the area we thought might have seen him. Many were nice enough to let us post flyers in and around their buildings.

We made several trips to the local animal shelter to check on whether any information on Marcel might have come to them. Unfortunately our plight only elicited sympathetic shoulder shrugs and headshakes, but no Marcel. The only bright moment at the shelter was when they knew immediately upon our saying we were looking for a Brussels Griffon what dog we were talking about. They had the flyers that had been sent out through the Stafford SPCA, and we were relieved to know that the process was working as advertised.

We experienced a horrifying moment while driving through the neighborhood when Beth and I saw an animal roughly the same size and with similar hair that had been hit on the road and was now not easily recognizable. Beth assured me that it was not Marcel, but I was not easily convinced until I had driven by enough times to verify that it could not be him.

As the day wore on with no results, Beth and I headed to my house. We were running out of steam and we were also running out of options. I finally lost my tenuous hold on my tears. There was an awkward silence in the car as I cried silently and Beth tried to pretend she didn't notice. I spoke muffled words through my tears because I sensed her silence was discomfort, "You don't have to say or do anything. I just need a few minutes. I'll be okay." She seemed relieved at this news, and blurted out, "I am not good with emotions. I don't do the hugging thing or really anything that involves tears or that sort of thing." She promptly ducked into texting and emailing. I didn't know if it was Michelle, another friend, or work. It didn't matter to me; I just needed a few minutes to come to terms with my own grief. Later it would become a point of humor for all of us to chuckle over.

Chapter 6

The HOV plan went flawlessly. After a quick round of well wishes from Tracy and her family, I was soon sitting shotgun in my own car, Bonnie driving while Ally fed me the to-go meal she had bought from Subway. Food had no taste and I nibbled what I could only for the nutrients I knew I needed.

We flew south on I-95 while the traffic in the environmentally-negligent lanes stood at a standstill that might very well have killed me had I been caught in it. We went straight to Karen's house, where she and Beth were just coming back to re-group and meet up with the fresh members of the day's search party. Karen's face spoke libraries and all we could do was hug and cry, which further added to Beth's discomfort.

As Michelle and I hugged and cried and started to discuss what had already been done and what we should do next, Isabel suddenly burst from the house with the news that there was a message on the answering machine about Marcel. We raced into the house to listen to the message. A man named Ed said he worked at the power plant down at the end of Possum Point Road. He had seen "our dog" at 4:30 the previous afternoon trotting along Possum Point near a yellow house and a truck repair shop and yard. He left his name and number for us to call him and get more information.

Beth and I had traversed Possum Point many times because we felt it was logical for Marcel to have ended up there based on the woods and what land was navigable and what was not. He would not have gone beyond where the road ended because the Potomac was there. We had made a point of stopping and talking to the men at the power plant and leaving a flyer with them.

Ed said he had not called sooner because, until he saw the flyer, he had no way of knowing the dog he had seen the day before was lost. The most comforting part of his description was he had noticed him trotting along with his little Air Force collar. We put Michelle on the phone right away to get as much information from Ed as possible. We learned that Ed had spotted Marcel literally 15 minutes after he bolted from the house. This meant that Marcel had run in a blind panic from the time he first bolted until he hit Possum Point Road. He covered approximately 1.5 to 2 miles of very rough terrain at a high speed. Ed's description of Marcel's attitude when he saw him along the road told us that by then Marcel had transitioned from blind panic into survival mode. This was good news, because it meant he would likely find an area to settle down and we would have a shot at finding him if we could just figure out what area he was likely spending most of his time.

The tip we got from Ed was the most promising news we'd had. His description of the yellow house—there was more than one on that road, but only one near a truck repair shop—helped us narrow down the location.

We thought it best to befriend the owners of the Yellow House, our new designated search hub. An impatient, "Do you have my dog?" was the first thing out of my mouth as I thrust one of the flyers in front of them.

"We don't even like dogs," they said. In fact, the mother said she was afraid of dogs.

I couldn't comprehend not liking dogs, but they were kind people sympathetic to my desperate predicament.

Meanwhile, Steve helped me find a dog tracker named Samantha, and while I had talked with her on the phone, I hadn't officially committed my credit card digits for her services. I updated Samantha on everything Karen and the search team was doing. Samantha said I didn't need her services because Karen was on point with all that should be done: I was wearing and then leaving shirts with a small bowl of food at feeding stations near Yellow House. Typically a modest person, I had no issues pulling off a shirt to leave it lying around for Marcel to smell his way back to me. By the evening, several of my shirts were strewn sporadically along Possum Point road.

Joining my niece Ally was the rest of her family—my sister Barb, my brother-in-law Ken and their other daughter Jess—who had made the 20-mile trek down to Dumfries from Springfield. Marcel had been missing for just over 24 hours and the amount of support I had in the search was tremendous. Ken, Barb, Jess, Ally, Karen, Beth, Bonnie and I had three separate vehicles and were able to fan out the search posse.

My sister and her family—my family—started on foot, wandering through the truck repair yard that shared a property line with Yellow House. Less a repair place than a pasture for the irreparable, the trucks were scattered about, providing, in my mind, a number of places for Marcel to hide. Perhaps he was in there, waiting to hear me calling for him.

When I had first gotten Marcel—an otherwise hyper-alert dog—his reactions or lack thereof, to some of our calls and noises made us suspect he might have had some hearing loss. He would usually respond to higher frequency "noises" and in trying to discover a pitch that would get his attention, I stumbled on a high pitched, albeit annoying "BEEP" that worked better than an alert siren did for recalling an aircrew to their jet. Worse than its piercing pitch was its two-syllable pronunciation. Poor Ken—my devoted niece Jess had her dad shed all facets of dignity in order to practice the "BE–EEP" during the 30-minute drive to Dumfries. And so we meandered through the truck infirmary, "BE-EEP" ing for Marcel.

Needing an escort for my numb self, Barb walked with me, praying out loud that the Lord bring Marcel out of hiding and back to me. Reassurance that this was somehow going to end well energized me. I still didn't know how, and I didn't know the exact definition of "well," but I sensed my boy was alive. But if he was alive and willing to come out, it wasn't happening there.

After nosing around the trucks, we decided to jump back in the cars and search the wider area that vehicular paws would allow. Everyone had their sections of ground to cover and we started slowly driving, randomly hollering out the window and then listening as if we would be able to hear the jingle of Marcel's tags over the relative roar of car engines.

Each member of the search team had designated search areas or stations. Robert was monitoring the Internet and the phone back at the house and relaying any relevant updates to me. We continued to have people calling to ask if there was anything they could do to help or just offering moral support. Some of the kids from Isabel's school even went home and dragged their parents out to search the neighborhood or the woods along the high ground afforded by the power lines in an effort to find Marcel.

Robert relayed a phone call from the Yellow House Family saying they thought they saw a brown furry animal in a storm sewer tunnel. We all sped back to the search hub. I ran out of the car as we all huddled to hear what the matron of the family had seen. She pointed across the street to the cement pipe that channeled water under a driveway. The neighborhood kids were all gathered around one side of the pipe opening, hunched over and peering in on what I presumed was my scared little pup, waiting for me to let him know it was safe to come out. One of the boys of the Yellow House Family volunteered to be our lead across the street. The mother handed him a rake, which we all took as extremely odd. I let her know that *my* boy would come when I called him. She cleared up the confusion with an abrupt, "No, the animal is drowned."

My heart plummeted out of my soul.

> When we first arrived at the yellow house I hung back a little. Two reasons, the first being I did not believe Marcel was the animal that they had found and secondly because I was watching Michelle and her response. I already knew from Robert's call that the animal the family had found was dead and I was worried about Michelle. Once we confirmed where we were to look I ordered Michelle to her car and told her I would go see what animal was in the water. If I turned out to be wrong there was no way I wanted Michelle to see Marcel like that because I knew the sight would haunt her for years to come.

Karen snapped to and ordered me back to the car to shield me from witnessing the discovery of an unsightly and lifeless Marcel. Ally stood at the open door with a comforting hand on my back as I was left to picture what the rest of the search party was witnessing first hand as the Yellow House Son reached into the drainage pipe and dragged out a soaking wet mass of dead brown fur. I couldn't believe that this was how it was going to end. Somewhere deep inside was an emotion almost like relief at the pending confirmation that it was Marcel, relief only in that I would have closure. Right behind that emotion was the walled off series of disturbing details that I could only imagine had been a part of Marcel's last couple days. But above all those thoughts and images was the still more hopeful conviction that this ordeal was going to end better than finding my boy as a drowned lifeless mass.

"It's a squirrel!" came the shout from across the street. A new, deeper relief poured through me, and a new sense of urgency to resume the search surfaced. There was no time to mourn the squirrel's passing, I had my own bundle of fur to find.

The search party rallied again and we used the last rays of daylight to make one more round to look for Marcel. But even with all the extra help and support, Wednesday wound down with no success. It was a dejected group that, one by one, called it quits for the evening.

After most people had left, I continued to lurk around the school athletic field where Marcel had initially disappeared from view. A few of my family and friends stayed with me and watched helplessly as I set up a lawn chair and tent, as I was intent on camping there to wait for Marcel to return to the scene of his departure. It was 9:30 pm and we all stood around and chatted casually...until the local police on his normal patrol route stopped by. It was then that I was informed (as Steve and Stephanie had already learned) that "hanging out" on school property well after normal school hours was illegal. My brother-in-law Ken, a former police officer, explained why we were there and bought us a little more time as the patrol policeman offhandedly let us know that he was on shift until 11 pm and probably wouldn't have the time to come back by the school during the rest of his shift.

So we continued to wait there for the next phase of what was rapidly becoming a full-scale paramilitary operation—Stephanie was on her way down to Dumfries with two pairs of night vision goggles, or "nogs" in military parlance.

My family and Karen took off to get some well-deserved rest, leaving Stephanie, Bonnie and I on the night shift. We loaded up into my car and cautiously, ever mindful of a brown furry critter scurrying across the street, drove back to Possum Point Road, where the lack of street lights made the nogs most useful. Already in a vigilant state of mind, the energy in the car buzzed with enthusiastic impatience. Bonnie drove slowly along the road while Stephanie and I scanned the woods and open fields with our eyes pressed into the small eyecups of the nogs.

Night vision goggles magnify any ambient light thousands of times, making every small movement detectable. My body's conditioned physiological response kicked in—my previous experiences with night vision goggles had been in combat environments when I was usually scanning for something dangerous. Peering through the night vision goggles brought back sensations I had when I had scanned desolate horizons in Afghanistan, Uzbekistan and Iraq. In combat scans, you weren't always sure of what it was you were scanning for, but you knew you'd know it when you saw it. The head-on-a-swivel visual sweep was a mostly boring task of looking for the "something," livened up by the possibility of seeing that something. Because I knew the something for which I scanned, I was uber-alert.

Through the nogs, the dark, undeveloped land along Possum Point Road became a bright, crisp green-hued field of possible Marcel sightings. Dragonflies darted along in the night, detectable only to Stephanie and me, easily tracking their flight. Bonnie kept a slow, steady pace along the road. We passed by a break in the trees, replaced by a rolling valley of high grass. Knowing our chances of seeing movement were even better without having to differentiate tree trunks or stumps from live animals, Stephanie and I gripped our night vision goggles tighter and focused our scan as we came along the open field. Then, we both saw it. A quick-moving animal, leaping through the grass. The small animal had an anxious gait.

"STOP!" we both yelled.

And, boy, did Bonnie stop. Her smooth driving was replaced by a reflexive stomp on the brakes, which sent both Stephanie and I slamming into our respective window frames through which we had been leaning.

Oblivious to the pain we should have felt, we threw open our doors and ran out of the car. We resumed our scan, alternating with naked eye and night vision goggle-assisted views. Bonnie deftly turned the car to shine the high beams into the field where we could see a lone deer, far enough away to have passed for a smaller animal, leaping through the grass. Ironically, the unusual presence of a car slowly pacing the road was probably what spooked the deer. As the emotional charge that came with the possible Marcel sighting diminished, we took our spots back in the car.

Bonnie resumed her route as we continued our scan. She broke the tense silence, glancing at me in the rear view mirror, "You know, it might double our chances of seeing Marcel if you two were looking out both sides of the car."

I looked to the empty back seat to my left just as I saw Stephanie reach for the door handle to vacate her shotgun seat and fill the spot. Just about the time Stephanie was realizing what I should have realized when we first started the night operation, we all started laughing as I sheepishly slid over to cover the left side of the car while Stephanie remained in the front seat covering the right side of the road. It was the first time I had laughed in the 30 hours since Marcel went missing.

The deer sighting was the only significant movement we caught with the nogs and after a couple hours we headed back to the school. It was nearing midnight and we were exhausted from the emotional seesaw of getting a tip that someone had seen him, then not finding him, hearing about an animal in the storm sewer, then learning it wasn't him, thinking we'd spotted him with the nogs, then realizing we hadn't. Weary from the day and the headache that comes with straining to see any movement through night vision goggles, we called it a night. Stephanie drove home while Bonnie caravanned us home in my car.

The ride was quiet as we travelled north on I-95, driving farther away from where I knew Marcel was. I shook my head, defeated. I had felt so strongly when I left Georgia that morning that I was going to find my boy. I could hardly fathom that I was riding away without him in my arms. I stared out the window, watching the sparse midnight traffic through a blur of tears.

I went to work on Thursday because I couldn't impose again upon the good nature of my bosses. My boss saw me shortly after I arrived and asked if we had found Marcel. Fighting back tears, I struggled to keep my face neutral as I shook my head. Without hesitation she asked, "What are you doing here? I know you want to go look for him. Go. Go now. You are going to find him, I just feel it." Flooded with relief at being able to leave and renewed energy to follow orders and continue searching for Marcel, I called Robert to come get me because there wouldn't be any buses home for several hours. Isabel was at school and this gave Robert and I much needed time to put together a plan.

We went home and printed out a Google Maps satellite view and went out in the car to systematically pinpoint barriers that would help us define Marcel's "hunker down" area. He was skittish enough that, no longer in panic mode, he was not likely to cross any main roads, nor go too close to highly populated areas. We had just made it home from this effort, and I finished making a new map of what I felt should be the new focus of the search when Michelle arrived.

I drove back down to Dumfries early Thursday afternoon. Samantha, the dog tracker I had finally hired, was coming down at 8:30 that night, after the peak temperatures had passed. While I hadn't given up, I was out of options. My boy had been missing for nearly 2 days. Dozens of people had searched on foot and by car. Hundreds of flyers were posted on telephone poles and in area animal shelters. Word had gone viral with online posts re-posted many times over. I felt as if doing the same thing was futile—it would only yield the same results.

Thinking that waiting for the professional dog tracker held the most success, I walked the field at the elementary school, pacing, hoping Marcel would come out if it was just me. I took the time to make the two phone calls I had yet to make and the two I dreaded the most: a call to Sabina, the owner of the Caring Hearts Rescue, the organization that had pulled Marcel from a life of confined filth and a call to Pat, Marcel's foster Mom who, despite having rescued more than 30 other dogs, endured the constant text and e-mail pictures I sent her of me and my boy in our first 29 days together. I sobbed into my cell phone as I confessed that I had failed the dog they had entrusted to me. They cried with me and joined in on the search, both using their well-established dog rescue networks to get the word out. Sabina even had contacts with the local news station and lined up a television news crew to come down at 8:30 to capture the dog tracker's hopefully successful search. If the search was unsuccessful, Sabina wanted my tearful, on-camera plea to entice more people to keep an eye out for Marcel. If I were to have a speaking role, subtitles would have been required.

But finally, knowing that Karen was released from work and was waiting for me at her house, I slowly made my way up to her place.

Michelle was not enthusiastic when she arrived. She was so discouraged. She said to me at that point she thought the only benefit to going out to look was that it would make us feel better to be doing something, but not because she thought we would find him. She was sure someone had him. We had had one false alarm along those lines the night before. I, on the other hand, was fairly certain that unless Marcel was unable to run from anyone trying to catch him, he was not likely to be caught.

At this point I was actually starting to feel optimistic. When Robert and I had mapped out the area, it was smaller than I thought originally, due to many natural (such as the river) and manmade boundaries. I felt certain that if Michelle and I could go out there, and slowly walk and call for him, that we would find him. I told Michelle I would be the navigator and an extra set of eyes, but that I would be silent while she called and "beeped" for Marcel. I did not tell her about my optimism, just in case I was wrong. The last thing she needed was another round of dashed hopes.

She and I headed out to search. We didn't need the extra people or added noise that might drive Marcel away, and we needed to move slowly enough that Marcel would have time to respond. Our plan was to walk in the area Robert and I had mapped out as the most likely area based on the Yellow House sighting and the boundaries that would prevent Marcel from leaving the area.

We left my house at 3:05 in the afternoon, closing in on 48-hours since Marcel had first dashed off, and headed to the beginning of our grid, which was not far from the Yellow House and truck yard. Slowly we walked, Michelle called and beeped while I listened, watched and kept us on track with the map. Suddenly we heard a high pitched barking that sounded a lot like it could have been Marcel coming from a house right around the corner from the truck yard. We raced across the street. We looked over the fence and saw nothing, but at this point the man that lived there came out and clearly was not pleased that we were peering into his yard.

Chapter 7

"You think I got your dog?" he stormed. "You wanna look in my back yard?"

"Kind of," I shrugged, but Karen kept my sarcasm in check as she mediated the man's defensiveness and my impatience.

"Look, my dad died and left me his incontinent terrier dog. The dog is 12 years old and chews stuff and pisses in the house so I have to keep him out here, I'm not letting it in my house," the man rattled off. In fact, he rattled the story off so quickly, I figured he couldn't have made it up on the spot. I started believing that he didn't have Marcel back there.

We explained what we were doing and why we were so anxious. He remembered Karen from the previous day when she was out putting up flyers. He was still defensive over us thinking he had our dog, but we managed to soothe him into realizing we didn't think he would do such a thing, that we were only following the sound of barking.

Tempered a bit by the man's explanation and the fact that it really didn't sound like Marcel's bark after all, I calmed down while Karen continued relaying our saga to the man. I was thankful when my cell phone rang so I could tend to the call and put off mending a relationship with this man that wasn't off to a great start.

"Hey, I'm calling about that dog," the caller said. My heart pounded. Plenty of unfamiliar numbers had shown up on my phone over the past couple of days, some to wish me good luck, some were friends of friends volunteering to help, some were useless calls to tell me they'd seen a spotted dog, or a black dog, or some dog bearing absolutely no resemblance to Marcel's picture.

"He's running down the road," the voice was excited and the excitement was contagious.

"Hey!" I interrupted Karen and man with an incontinent, inherited terrier, disregarding every lesson I had learned about not interrupting unless it was necessary and then doing it with manners, "Someone sees him!"

"What road?" I asked the caller, ready to sprint toward the sighting even if it was in another county.

"Possum Point."

I grabbed the satellite view map Karen held in her hands to confirm what I was already pretty sure about; we were *on* Possum Point Road. I took off, not even sure if I was heading the right way.

"I'm going to get your car," Karen yelled after me. Good thing because I couldn't remember where she had parked it and wasn't in a proper emotional state to drive a motor vehicle anyway.

I got the rest of the details about where Marcel was running while I panted into the phone during my sprint. I was wearing jeans and hiking shoes to protect my legs from the tick-infested brambles we had been trudging through, and was still wearing multiple shirts so I could continue displaying my T-shirt wardrobe at random points around Dumfries. Suffice it to say, that with temperatures above 103 and my emotional state running even hotter, it was a sticky sprint.

My eyes scanned the asphalt that stretched out in front of me. There were no sidewalks along Possum Point, just a thin strip of dirt that demarcated road from woods. As I ran, my cell phone announced another unfamiliar caller and then another. Marcel was out and still running along Possum Point Road. I was close. Adrenaline coursed through my body, moving my legs faster than they'd ever run.

I sensed a car stalking me and turned to see Karen eagerly following behind the wheel of my car. As I ran alongside my own car, I watched an oncoming car screech to a halt as its passenger jumped out and ripped one of our "Lost Dog" signs off the stop sign post.

"HEY!" I yelled across the street, appalled at actually catching a sign stealer. We had re-visited places and posts where we had put up signs only to find them removed. "What are you doing?!?!"

"I see this dog!" the lady hollered as she shook Marcel's sign.

"That's MY DOG!" I yelled back. Now my heart was racing. If I was looking at the person who had seen him, I knew he was close.

"He's running right down the street, running that way," she pointed in the same direction I had been running. Marcel and I were both running to find each other but just not toward each other!

"Get in the car!" Karen ordered. I complied even though I was positive I could have outrun any car.

The car that had previously violated Possum Point Road speed limits to steal the sign to call me and tell me of their sighting, fell in behind us, flashing their hazard lights to stall traffic that got behind them. Karen kept a steady pace and we both hunched over the dashboard trying to get that much closer to seeing Marcel.

And then we saw him.

He was trotting along the road, right in the middle of the little dirt strip as if it was meant for his little paws. If this had been a cartoon, he would have had a little dog-sized hobo pack slung over his shoulder. His pace was skittish but determined and his gait a little unsteady. But there he was. I couldn't believe it.

I pawed at the door handle to get out and get him back in my arms.

Karen knew better and just as I edged into hyperactive mode, she settled in to ultra-composed mode. "Stay," she commanded, the five fingers of her right hand clawed my left shoulder, as she divided her attention between controlling me and keeping the car from hitting Marcel should he decided to stray from his path.

I wanted to get to Marcel. I could see him, and barring any catastrophic car accidents, he was seconds away from being in my arms. But Karen had a hold of me and I realized she was trying to make sure we didn't spook him into running again.

"Roll down your window," Karen said calmly. I did.

"Call his name," she said.

"Marcel," I cried timidly. His ears perked up but he only barely acknowledged our presence. He was tired, hungry, thirsty, scared and still lost. I was afraid he was going to bolt again. I waited for my next command from Karen, unsure of when I should get out of the car.

We crept alongside Marcel. I could tell from Karen's pace that we would aim to get ahead of him.

"Call his name again," she said as the car passed by Marcel. He turned and looked at the car and for the first time in 48 hours, I was looking at my boy's face, not at his picture, at his *actual* face.

Karen brought the car to a stop. Marcel stopped too.

"Slowly open the door," she said. I did, doing my best with the "slowly" part.

"Get out of the car." I did.

Marcel looked at me and his entire face changed. In a moment, I saw recognition and relief replace the fear and fatigue in his eyes.

"Call him," Karen said. I did.

And at 3:37 pm, 32 minutes after we had left Karen's house, I called him and that little boy leapt into my arms. I stood up, incredulous that I was actually holding him, refusing to let go. He had sharp burrs embedded throughout his coat and was panting from the heat, but he licked my face enthusiastically at our reunion. We were lucky enough to find each other once, but surely we had expended our luck by finding each other a second time.

When I realized that this ordeal was over, I sobbed. Tears of sorrow, joy, relief, love and gratitude, for the fear Marcel must have felt over the past 48 hours, for the loss of Q-Tip 2 months earlier, for the graciousness of friends and family who had put their lives on hold to look for Marcel and for the emotional toll we had all been through.

I looked up to see that there were cars backed up in both directions, the first few in each line actually watched the reunion unfold before them. The lady in the car behind us was crying, as was the couple in the car behind them. I carried Marcel back through the line so the first car could see the lost dog up close and so the second and third cars could see what the holdup was.

I was beyond exuberant and yet in tears from the relief of finding Marcel. I wanted to hug Marcel too but knew that the only thing he needed was Michelle so I did not even try. I just called Robert and blubbered out the good news. Robert was so happy and relieved at the news that he started to cry too. Up to this moment he had kept his emotions in check and focused on what needed to be done so even though I knew he felt terrible about Marcel's escape, it was not until that moment when I realized the depth of his grief over the events.

Karen was across the street calling Robert as the news began to spread beyond Possum Point Road. I snapped a picture, me with Marcel in my arms, and e-mailed it to work, posted it to Facebook and texted it to my family and friends.

I called Samantha, the dog tracker, with four hours to spare before she and her dog started their trek down the I-95 corridor to help us.

"Samantha, I just wanted to let you know you don't need to come down tonight. We just found Marcel along the road."

"Oh, I am so sorry to hear that," sympathy oozed through the phone.

I was confused that she didn't share my joy, thinking uncharitably that perhaps she was mourning lost profits from what was going to be an expensive part in my search for Marcel. Then I suddenly understood and clarified, "No no no, we just found Marcel *walking* along the road!"

Her response was much more upbeat and I realized she wasn't in the job for the money, she was in it for the reunions. "That's fantastic! Congratulations!!!!"

Michelle and I were so worried about Marcel's condition after his ordeal that I suggested we go straight to my vet just two miles away. I called and explained the situation and they got us right in. Fortunately aside from burrs, a little dehydration, and hunger Marcel was in good shape. Nothing food, water, and a bath could not fix.

During the visit to Karen's vet, I refused to be out of contact with Marcel for even a moment, either holding him or petting him constantly. I made sure he knew that I wasn't letting him out of my sight anytime soon.

The vet tech was kind enough to work out the burr souvenirs Marcel had collected over the past couple days and we walked out with a re-hydrated, de-burred dog and a bag of antibiotics.

Chapter 8

We all went back to Karen's house so Robert and Marcel could be reunited too. We gave Marcel a nice bath, but then I felt like I had invaded so much of Karen and Robert's family time over the past few days that I was in a rush to leave. When Karen insisted I stay, I thought she was just being polite, but she said she needed to spend some time where she could see Marcel so she could heal too. That, I understood. We ordered sushi and ate standing in the kitchen while we all stared, mesmerized by the little brown dog curled up on the floor, catching up on the sleep he had forgone for two days.

After we gave Marcel a bath, Michelle said she felt like she needed to leave because she didn't want to impose any further. I asked her to stay for dinner but she was still hesitant, knowing we were all exhausted. We were, but at the same time the reality of actually having Marcel safely found had not fully sunk in for Robert, Isabel, and me. I told Michelle that if she was not too tired that she would be doing us a favor if she stayed to eat. It would give us much needed time to absorb the fact that Marcel was indeed safe. I could tell she understood and, with no further hesitation, she agreed to dinner.

We stood around the kitchen island. Between eating and talking, we stared at the sleeping Marcel. He was curled up on the towel we had used to dry him after his bath. It took about an hour to really absorb that we had indeed found him. He was so exhausted that he was oblivious to being stared at by four pairs of eyes that could barely look away to grab another bite of dinner. By the time we finished dinner and got Michelle and Marcel on the road, we were starting to relax. I knew that for the first time since this had started, we would finally be able to sleep.

It was—and still is—difficult to fully express in words the sheer joy, relief, and gratefulness that swirled around competing with the remnants of wondering "what if?" What could we have done so this had never happened? What if we had not found him? What if we had gone straight to Possum Point Road and just camped there? Would we have found him sooner? In the end the happy thoughts chased away the questions and life gradually returned to normal.

A few hours later, I was driving home, just Marcel and me in the car. I struggled to keep my eyes on the road, tempted to keep staring at my boy snuggled up in my lap. As I pulled into my driveway, there were welcome home signs and balloons on my garage door made and signed by my neighbors!

I gave Marcel one more bath then laid with him in bed just as the weather that had been predicted for the evening rolled in with all the fury of a summer thunderstorm. Heavy rain, blinding flashes of lightning and pounding booms of thunder filled the humid air. I protected Marcel in my arms as he snored, unfazed by the noises.

The storm held off just long enough. Had it come before we had found Marcel, it would have erased his scent, reducing the probability of the dog tracker finding him. And of course, if it had come while he was still missing, I would have ached even more with the fear of his being alone in the woods enduring the storm. But with him in my arms, I didn't care if the storm ripped the roof from my home because it couldn't tear the dog from my arms.

Chapter 9

When we started writing this story, we thought the only readers who would understand were those who had connected deeply with an animal or pet. But I think all of us have connected with someone, be it a pet or person, so profoundly that they became a part of you.

I wanted to share these experiences for several reasons. The first was catharsis. It was such a powerfully wrenching series of events with such great emotional impact not only for me, but for Karen, all those who helped, and even the lady in the car behind us with her hazard lights on to hold up traffic.

The second reason is in the story itself—the kind of drama that movies are made of, with, as in a Shakespeare play, unforeseeable events, crossed communications, mistaken identities, sudden reversals, heroic interventions and the occasional comic relief.

Third, I wanted to publicly recognize and give thanks for the truly staggering love and support my friends and family—*Marcel's* friends and family—have shown me from the moment of Q-Tip's fatal encounter with the big dog to the outpouring of joy as the word spread of Marcel's return. I owe so much gratitude not only to Karen and Robert, but to our respective bosses, the close friends who were up all night, the huge net of people who reached out through Facebook, the SPCA and the foster organization and those strangers in Dumfries who went out of their way to contact a person they'd never met in a moment of need. We think these days that Good Samaritans are a dying breed, but from Ed at the power plant, to the policeman who let us keep our vigil, to the woman afraid of dogs who nevertheless helped us search for one, to the one who broke every traffic rule to get the news of her sighting to us...we found them everywhere.

And finally, I wanted to share the richness of a life with dogs, and my conviction that we don't own them—they own us. In this story of dog-love found, lost, regained, lost, and found again, I realize again how fortunate I have been to share that deep connection with not one, but two four-legged friends.

My life would have had fewer agonizing moments, fewer tears, and less heartbreak, without Q-Tip and Marcel—but I would have been so much poorer for their absence. I have had, and I hope will continue to have for many, many years to come, the blessing that is the unconditional love of a dog.

I wish the same for you.